EDGE
BOOKS™

Secret America

Secret American People

From Secret Societies to Secret Agents

by Christopher Forest

Consultant:
Jessica Martin, PhD
History Department
University of Colorado, Boulder

Capstone
press®

Mankato, Minnesota

Edge Books are published by Capstone Press,
151 Good Counsel Drive, P.O. Box 669, Mankato, Minnesota 56002.
www.capstonepress.com

Books published by Capstone Press are manufactured with paper
containing at least 10 percent post-consumer waste.

Library of Congress Cataloging-in-Publication Data
Forest, Christopher.
    Secret American people: from secret societies to secret agents / by
Christopher Forest.
    p. cm. — (Edge. Secret America)
    Summary: "Describes a variety of secret and mysterious people in the
United States" — Provided by publisher.
    Includes bibliographical references and index.
    ISBN: 978-1-4296-3361-1 (library binding)
    1. Secret societies — United States — Juvenile literature. 2. Secrecy
— United States — Miscellanea — Juvenile literature. 3. Spies — United
States — Juvenile literature. 4. Curiosities and wonders — United States —
Juvenile literature. I. Title.
HS204.F67 2010
366.0973 — dc22   2009003330

Editorial Credits

Kathryn Clay, editor; Tracy Davies, designer; Eric Gohl, media researcher

Photo Credits
Alamy/picturebox-uk.com, cover (right), 23 (top), 28; AP Images, 15; AP
Images/Alex Brandon, 16; AP Images/Gerald Herbert, 13; AP Images/The News
Tribune, Peter Haley, 11; AP Images/Ron Edmonds, 17; Capstone Press/Karon
Dubke, cover (left), 24; George Bush Presidential Library, cover (middle),
12; Getty Images Inc., 25; Getty Images Inc./AFP/Paul J. Richards, 18; Getty
Images Inc./The Bridgeman Art Library, 7; Getty Images Inc./Charles Ommanney,
20; Getty Images Inc./The Image Bank/Andy Caulfield, 26; Getty Images Inc./
Vintage Images, 14; Jake Dobkin/Streetsy.com, 27; Landov LLC/Dennis Brack, 23
(bottom); Library of Congress, 6, 8; Shutterstock/Cobalt Moon Design,
(patriotic background design element); Shutterstock/digitalife, (banners
design element); Shutterstock/Janaka, (paper design element); Shutterstock/
jirkaejc, 19; Shutterstock/Paul Paladin, 9; Shutterstock/PKruger, (cobbled
road design element); Shutterstock/Sergey Kandakov, (black paper design
element); Shutterstock/Sibrikov Valery, (old paper design element);
Shutterstock/Stijn Boelens, cover (background), 4; Shutterstock/velora,
(wax seal design element)

Table of Contents

Keeping Secrets

They hide in underground tunnels and meet behind locked doors. They use fake names and work undercover.

America is filled with mysterious people. Did you know that many founding fathers were members of secret societies like the Freemasons? Even some of today's leaders are members of the Skull and Bones.

Sometimes organizations are well known, but their activities are top secret. Every day we count on members of the Central Intelligence Agency (CIA) to keep our country safe. But few people understand just how they do it.

Because the groups are so mysterious, they raise a lot of questions. Who can join them? Why do they exist? And why do they insist on being so secretive? Get ready to learn the truth about the secret people in America.

The Sons of Liberty

Members of the Sons of Liberty felt the British taxes were unfair.

In 1765, America was part of Great Britain. When Britain needed more money, the king taxed the American **colonists**. The colonists did not want to pay the new taxes.

Storekeepers and artists from Boston hoped to put an end to the taxes. They were known as the Loyal Nine. Word of the group spread, and more people wanted to join. The group then became known as the Sons of Liberty.

Being part of the Sons of Liberty was dangerous. The group met in secret so they wouldn't get caught. Some members committed **treason**. They damaged British cargo ships and spoke out against the government. The punishment for treason was death.

The Sons of Liberty convinced many colonists to fight against British laws. Disagreements between colonists and British rulers eventually led to the Revolutionary War (1775–1783).

Edge Fact:
Famous patriots Paul Revere and Samuel Adams were members of the Sons of Liberty.

colonist — someone who lives in a newly settled area

treason — the act of betraying your country

The Boston Tea Party

The Sons of Liberty wanted to protest the Tea Act passed in 1773. In December 1773, they boarded three ships that carried tea from Britain. Disguised as American Indians, they dumped more than 300 chests of tea into the Boston Harbor.

The Freemasons

Members of the Freemasons wear special costumes during important events.

Edge Fact:

The Freemasons have about 5 million members throughout the world.

After the American colonists won the Revolutionary War, there were important choices to make. What would the new government be like? Who would lead the country? Many leaders stepped forward with answers. Some of these leaders, like Benjamin Franklin and George Washington, belonged to a secret group called the Freemasons.

The Freemasons are a very old society. Most people agree that a group of **stonemasons** started the organization in London in 1717. Others argue that the group is much older. We do know that English immigrants brought the group with them to the United States.

stonemason — someone who builds or works with stone

Secret Symbols

Look closely at the back of a dollar bill. You'll see a pyramid and an eye. These designs are similar to Freemason symbols. That's because some of the leaders responsible for choosing national symbols were Freemasons. They picked familiar images. The pyramid and the eye symbolize that the United States is still unfinished.

The American Freemasons helped to establish the United States. In fact, 13 signers of the U.S. Constitution were Freemasons. The Declaration of Independence was also signed by several Freemasons.

Despite their important role in American history, Freemasons are still considered very mysterious. Their meetings are open only to members. They share secret passwords and handshakes.

Members participate in **rituals** called Masonic degrees. These ceremonies are held in special lodges and include music, costumes, and props.

The mysteries surrounding the Freemasons have some people very concerned. They worry that the Freemasons have too much power in the government. A few people even believe they are trying to take over the world.

Freemasons consider themselves private but not secret. They do not hide the fact that they are members. Yet few people know what actually happens behind the closed doors of their lodges.

ritual — an action that is always performed in the same way

Edge Fact:

Former U.S. presidents Theodore Roosevelt, Harry Truman, and Ronald Reagan were all Freemasons.

Freemasons pose with their medals at the Prince Hall Masonic Temple in Tacoma, Washington.

Skull and Bones Society

Bonesmen chosen in 1948 included former U.S. President George H. W. Bush (left of clock).

The Skull and Bones Society is one of the oldest and most secretive groups in America. Its members are called Bonesmen. They meet in a windowless building nicknamed the Tomb.

In 1832, students at Yale University in New Haven, Connecticut, started the Skull and Bones Society. Each year, some of the most successful students at Yale are invited to join. In turn, their members have become very successful judges, politicians, and businesspeople. Maybe that's because members promise to help each other succeed. Bonesmen help other members get jobs and leadership positions.

Women are now allowed to be Bonesmen. Other than that, little has changed since the group formed. Each year, 15 people are invited to join during a nighttime ceremony. Members are given special nicknames.

A recent lawsuit claims that Geronimo's skull is kept in a glass box inside the Tomb. The great-grandson of the Apache warrior said Bonesmen stole the skull. According to legend, one of the robbers was Prescott Bush, the father of former president George H. W. Bush.

Famous Bonesmen

Some people worry about how much power the Bonesmen have. That's because many Bonesmen have held important government positions. In fact, three former U.S. presidents were Bonesmen. They are George H. W. Bush, George W. Bush, and William Taft.

The Mob

Mobsters were known for attacking their enemies with automatic weapons.

Edge Fact:

The Mob is also called the Mafia.

14

On February 14, 1929, gunfire rang out in the streets of Chicago. Members of Al Capone's gang raided a warehouse. They shot and killed members of the Bugs Moran gang. Known as the St. Valentine's Day Massacre, this is one of many events that have made the Mob famous.

The Mob is a system of organized crime. For more than 100 years, mobsters have operated in America's largest cities. When alcohol was illegal during the 1920s, the Mob made money by selling alcohol secretly. During the 1940s, the Mob opened casinos in Las Vegas. Now the Mob is involved in many activities including illegal weapon and drug sales.

What remains a mystery to most people is how mobsters manage to get away with their crimes. They do whatever they can to stay out of jail. Some hire hit men to commit murders. Others bribe police officers and threaten judges. And some mobsters simply kill anyone who gets in their way.

The Most Famous Mobster

Al Capone became a feared Mob boss by killing off his enemies. He was never charged with murder, but he was sent to prison for not paying his taxes. He suffered from an illness while in jail. By the time he was released, Capone was too ill to lead organized crime.

The Secret Service

Secret Service agents closely guard the president and his family against attackers.

Look carefully the next time the president speaks at an event. You might see people wearing dark suits and earpieces. They don't take their eyes off the crowd. They are members of the Secret Service.

In 1894, Secret Service agents protected President Grover Cleveland from an **assassination** attempt. Agents became full-time presidential bodyguards in 1901 after President William McKinley was assassinated.

Since then, the Secret Service has had two jobs — investigation and protection. Some agents investigate crimes that involve money and computers. Other agents protect the president. They also guard presidential families, former presidents, and visiting foreign leaders.

Like law enforcement agents, Secret Service agents carry guns and handcuffs. They wear radios and bulletproof vests. If the president plans to travel, the Secret Service makes sure a location is secure before the president arrives.

True to its name, most of the agency's work remains secret. By revealing few details, the Secret Service can better protect the president.

Edge Fact:
Agents use code names for the people they protect. President Obama's code name is "Renegade."

assassination — the murder of someone who is well known or important

A Dangerous Job

Protecting the president is a dangerous job. In 1981, agent Tim McCarthy was wounded while protecting President Ronald Reagan from a gunman. Agent Leslie Coffelt was killed in 1950 when someone tried to shoot President Harry Truman. Coffelt is the only agent to be killed while preventing an attack.

Tim McCarthy

The National Security Agency

Workers at the National Security Agency use computers to crack secret enemy codes.

The National Security Agency (NSA) is a secretive group with a complicated mission. For years, no one knew much about the NSA. People claimed the group didn't exist. They joked that NSA stood for "No Such Agency." But the NSA does exist, and its job is top secret.

Top Technology

The NSA has the fastest computers in the world. One NSA computer can manage 64 billion instructions each second. The NSA built the Tordella Supercomputer Building to hold the computers.

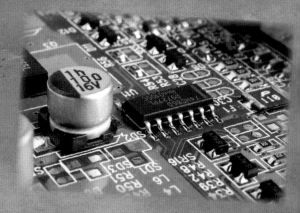

In 1952, President Harry Truman created the NSA to keep track of foreign enemies. NSA workers cracked codes used during the Korean War (1950–1953) and during the Vietnam War (1954–1975).

Today workers collect information on suspected terrorists using high-tech computer systems. NSA workers listen to private conversations and gather foreign information that is usually written in code. NSA workers crack these secret codes so government leaders can use the information.

All the secrecy makes some people nervous — and with good reason. Recent reports show that the NSA might be keeping watch on American citizens. This includes recording millions of phone calls and e-mails. But no one knows just how much information the agency may have collected.

Edge Fact:
Technology invented by the NSA was used to develop computers and cassette tapes.

The Central Intelligence Agency

Their jobs are some of the most secretive and the most dangerous. They travel the world undercover to gather secret information. They are spies for the Central Intelligence Agency (CIA).

The CIA was created in 1947 to collect **intelligence** in foreign countries. During the 1960s, the CIA gathered information that kept dangerous weapons out of foreign countries. CIA spies also collected information that helped U.S. soldiers fighting in the Vietnam War (1954–1975). Today the CIA gathers information on everything from suspected terrorists to mobsters and illegal drug dealers.

Edge Fact:

More than 10,000 people apply to work for the CIA each month.

intelligence — secret information about an enemy's plans or actions

CIA Requirements

Not just anyone can be a CIA agent. Recruits must be U.S. citizens. They need to go to college and get good grades. They have to pass a lie detector test and medical tests. Agents also must be willing to move to Washington, D.C., or to foreign countries.

CIA spies work in the United States and in foreign countries. They have many ways to collect information. Spies check foreign newspapers, TV reports, and radio broadcasts. Some spies use satellites to watch foreign leaders.

Undercover spies must create false identities. They have fake names, birthdays, and life histories. They use makeup and disguises to change their appearance.

Not all CIA workers collect top secret information, though. Some spies are responsible for protecting government secrets. These people work with the Federal Bureau of Investigation (FBI) to keep military secrets out of enemy hands. This is called **counterintelligence**. Sometimes enemies are even given false information. The CIA hopes the phony information will confuse enemies.

counterintelligence — actions designed to keep secrets safe from enemies

Edge Fact:
The president receives an update from the CIA each morning called the President's Daily Brief.

Spy Gear

Spies have many high-tech tools to help them collect information. Photos are captured using cameras hidden in jewelry, buttons, or shoes. Tiny listening devices called bugs can be hidden just about anywhere. Bugs transmit conversations to recording devices.

Men in Black

Late at night, a strange light appears in the sky. A man calls the police to report an Unidentified Flying Object (UFO). Days later, three men wearing sunglasses and dark suits arrive at the man's door. They warn him not to talk about the UFO. This sounds like a Hollywood movie. But some people believe stories like this are very real.

Albert Bender was the first person to talk about the Men in Black (MIB). Bender ran a research group in Connecticut called the Flying Saucer Bureau. In 1953, he suddenly ended the group and his research. Bender later said that men in dark suits had visited him. They claimed to be government workers and insisted he stop investigating UFOs. Bender said the men told him the truth about UFOs. But he never said what that truth was.

In the 1960s, many people reported similar visits. Some people say MIB agents have gray skin and wires coming out of their legs. Other people think MIB agents are really aliens. If the Men in Black do exist, no one knows who, or what, they really are.

Edge Fact:
Several people claim that Men in Black have a tool that can erase memory.

Invading Hollywood

Men in Black are featured in many Hollywood movies. Actors Will Smith and Tommy Lee Jones played MIB agents in *Men in Black* and *Men in Black II*. Just like in reported MIB stories, these on-screen agents try to quiet people who claim to have seen UFOs.

The Mole People

Times Square
42 Street Station
A C E N R S
1 2 3 9 7

Open:
Monday–Friday
7:30am–10pm

Other times:
Enter across 42 St
or across 7 Av

Thousands of mole people might live in the
subway tunnels below New York City streets.

Some people claim that deep below New York
City is a secret world. They estimate more than
5,000 people live underground in the city's empty
subway tunnels. These secret citizens are called
the mole people.

The Freedom Tunnel

One New York City subway tunnel is called the Freedom Tunnel. The tunnel was named after graffiti artwork that Chris "Freedom" Pape painted throughout the tunnel. The tunnel opened in the 1930s but closed soon after. Then the first mole people moved in. In 1991, the tunnel was reopened for train usage. People who lived in the tunnel were forced to leave.

Many mole people are men who live alone in the tunnels. Some of them suffer from drug addiction or mental illness. They might stay underground for weeks at a time.

Edge Fact:

Some mole people use leaky pipes to get water for drinking and cooking.

Other mole people may simply be happier living away from the noisy city life. They might go to school or have jobs aboveground.

It's possible some mole people have lived underground for more than 10 years. They may have formed communities of leaders, teachers, and nurses.

Life in the tunnels can be difficult and extremely dangerous. Gangs, lack of medicine, and fights with other mole people cause problems. But this hasn't stopped them from making a home beneath the city.

Uncovering New Secrets

This book has listed a few of the secret people in America, but there are countless others. Some groups are well known. The Bilderberg Club is thought to have a huge influence on business. Other groups might be so secret that we don't even know they exist.

Now it's your turn to search for America's mysterious people. Check out the newspaper for organizations meeting in your neighborhood. Search the library for books on secret organizations. You might be amazed by all the secret people around you.

Glossary

assassination (uh-sass-uh-NAY-shun) — the murder of someone who is well-known or important

colonist (KAH-luh-nist) — someone who lives in a newly settled area

counterintelligence (koun-tur-in-TEL-uh-jenss) — actions of an intelligence agency designed to protect secret information from enemies

graffiti (gruh-FEE-tee) — pictures drawn or words written on the walls of buildings or other surfaces

intelligence (in-TEL-uh-jenss) — secret information about an enemy's plans or actions

patriot (PAY-tree-uht) — an American colonist who disagreed with British rule of the American colonies

ritual (RICH-oo-uhl) — an action that is always performed in the same way

stonemason (STONE-may-suhn) — someone who builds or works with stone

treason (TREE-zuhn) — the crime of betraying your country

Read More

Farndon, John. *Do Not Open*. New York: DK, 2007.

O'Shei, Tim. *Spy Basics*. Spies. Mankato, Minn.: Capstone Press, 2008.

Southwell, David, and Sean Twist. *Secret Societies*. Mysteries and Conspiracies. New York: Rosen, 2008.

Internet Sites

FactHound offers a safe, fun way to find Internet sites related to this book. All of the sites on FactHound have been researched by our staff.

Here's all you do:

Visit *www.facthound.com*

FactHound will fetch the best sites for you!

Index